The First Pup

The Real Story of How Bo Got to the White House

Bob Staake

FEIWEL AND FRIENDS
NEW YORK

Once upon a time, a man named Barack Obama decided to run for president of the United States, and the most amazing thing happened...

he *won!*

The country was very happy and hoped that he would be a good president.

On the night of his victory, President Obama thanked the American voters and assured the world that he would work hard.

He then made another big announcement: Once his family had moved to their new home in Washington, D.C., his daughters, Sasha and Malia, would get . . .

a puppy!!!

Everyone shouted, applauded, and smiled—
but nobody was smiling more . . .

than Sasha and Malia.

The family went to Washington, D.C., and the entire world watched as Barack Obama was inaugurated as the first African-American president in the history of the United States.

The Obamas were now the nation's First Family.

There were people celebrating everywhere, and a long parade that began at the Capitol Building and ended at Sasha and Malia's new home . . . the White House!

The girls ran excitedly through the front doors. They couldn't WAIT to see their new puppy!

good luck mr prez

They saw television crews and chefs and generals and reporters and men with walkie talkies. They looked this way and that way and down here and up there—but there was no puppy—anywhere!

After a night of toasts, handshakes, music, food, and dancing at a dozen inaugural celebrations within the city, the First Family was ready to sleep in their big new home.

They slept soundly as the full moon passed over the Capitol, the Washington Monument, the White House, and finally set over the Lincoln Memorial.

In the morning, Sasha and Malia burst into their parents' room with stacks of books about dogs.

There were poodles and schnauzers and terriers and boxers!
Retrievers and Labradors and spaniels and collies!
There were Chihuahuas and shepherds and corgis and beagles!
Great Danes and dachshunds and dalmatians and huskies!

How could they ever choose just one?!

Meanwhile, far away on a farm in Texas, a puppy had been born only a month before President Obama's victory. He was a black Portuguese water dog with white markings. He looked like he was wearing a tuxedo! He was lively and smart and one of nine brothers and sisters. All of the pups found homes in different parts of the country. One even went to live with Senator Ted Kennedy in Washington, D.C.

But the lively little puppy didn't get along in the home he was sent to, so he came back to the Texas farm.

Poor puppy! What would happen to him now?

Back in Washington, D.C., Senator Kennedy knew that the president still hadn't found the right dog for his family. The senator also knew that Malia was allergic to most dogs, but that Portuguese water dogs are hypoallergenic.

When he learned that one of the litter of pups of his own new dog had been returned to the farm and needed a second chance, he had a great idea. . . .

On Easter weekend, there was a sudden frenzy of activity around the White House. The First Family gathered on the South Lawn.

The East Gate opened and a parade of motorcycles escorted
a long black limousine that stopped alongside a red carpet.
Then the door of the limousine opened and out stepped . . .

a puppy!

The black dog with white markings sat confused for a second, but when he saw the First Family at the end of the red carpet, his tail started wagging, his tongue hung out, and he ran to them with President Obama down the long red carpet.

Helicopters whirled in circles above! Television cameras filmed from high in the sky! Reporters called their newspapers! Web sites around the world instantly posted photos! Spectators along the White House's iron fence cheered wildly!

Sasha and Malia hugged and petted the little dog.

The news was official: The First Family now had its First Pup!

The president and the
First Lady made the girls
promise to feed the puppy,
give it exercise, and take
care of it on a daily basis.

But the president assured them that one
of the hardest parts was yet to come:
The girls would have to pick the perfect
NAME for the puppy!

Sasha and Malia already had that figured out. Their cousin's cat was named Bo, their grandfather's nickname was Diddley after the singer Bo Diddley, and their father and grandfather's initials were B.O.

Of course, their new puppy
would be named . . .

Bo!

The First Pup didn't much care about names.

He was just happy to be home—

on his first day,
in the First House,
with America's First Family.